T0145132

Granny's
APRONS

HOLLY WILLIAMS

Granny's Aprons

iUniverse books may be ordered through booksellers or by contacting:

iUniverse
1663 Liberty Drive
Bloomington, IN 47403
www.iuniverse.com
1-800-Authors (1-800-288-4677)

ISBN: 978-1-5320-8827-8 (sc)
ISBN: 978-1-5320-8829-2 (hc)
ISBN: 978-1-5320-8828-5 (e)

Library of Congress Control Number: 2019921163

Print information available on the last page.

iUniverse rev. date: 01/03/2020

Granny's
APRONS

My book is titled "Granny's Aprons"

Written for all those grannies around the world who wore or wear aprons and the many professions that wear them today.

Many grannies have worn an apron. Aprons come in all different shapes, sizes, colors and materials.

The definition of an apron from Webster's dictionary states"
a piece of cloth worn in front to protect your clothes."

Whatever apron your granny chose to wear–
she probably did a lot while wearing it.

Granny would teach me to bake bread,

make delicious meals,

wipe your tears if you were crying,
dusting the furniture, doing laundry,

rocking the baby,
play music,

work in the garden,

and even dance
around the house

Apron pockets can hold a lot of things. Granny's apron pockets had safety pins, pencil, note pad, peppermint candy, bandaids, chewing gum, clothes pins and many other things.

Can you name more things in granny's apron pockets?

1. _____
2. _____
3. _____
4. _____
5. _____

Granny would wear a beautiful flowery apron as she prepared Sunday dinner.

Granny wore her aprons
proudly, she also made them
and gave them as gifts.

Aprons are worn by many people while doing their jobs.

For example, a restaurant server,

a chef, a cook,

a barista,

a handyperson with
tools needed,

a gardener,

an art teacher

Can you name some people that wear aprons:

1. _____
2. _____
3. _____
4. _____
5. _____

Can you draw yourself an apron?

The end.

Special Thanks:

To my late father, Joe Brown Sr. for giving me physical life and life lessons, to my mother Shirley for giving me a strong sense of family love, family values... for entrusting me with many family photos and keepsakes that date back to the 1800s, to my brother Joe and my sister Lori for their love and support throughout my whole life, to my brother Victor, sisters Myrtle and (gone to soon) Yvette, to my brother-in-laws, Donald (Lori) and Chris(Myrtle). To my wonderful children, James and Camille and thank you to their dad Jimmy for two beautiful children and a stepdaughter Tahirah, to my granddaughters Shaniya and Jayda and to all my family, friends and illustrator (Olivia) who have contributed their knowledge and expertise through-out the book writing process.

Printed in the United States
By Bookmasters